Circle of Compassion

Meditations for Caring—

For the Self and the World

Gail Straub

Journey Editions   BOSTON • TOKYO • SINGAPORE

First published in 2001 by Journey Editions, an imprint of Periplus Editions (HK) Ltd, with editorial offices at 153 Milk Street, Boston, Massachusetts 02109.

Library of Congress Cataloging-in-Publication Data

Straub, Gail.
    Circle of compassion : meditations for caring for self and the world / Gail Straub.--
1st ed.
        p. cm.
    ISBN 1-58290-044-2 (pbk.)
        1. Conduct of life. 2. Caring. 3. Affirmations. I. Title.

BF637.C5 S717 2001
158.1'28--dc21   2001029105

Distributed by:

North America
Tuttle Publishing
Distribution Center
Airport Industrial Park
364 Innovation Drive
North Clarendon, VT
05759-9436
Tel: (802) 773-8930
Toll free tel: (800) 526-2778
Fax: (802) 773-6993
Toll free fax: (800) 329-8885

Japan
Tuttle Publishing
RK Bldg. 2nd Floor
2-13-10 Shimo-Meguro
Meguro-Ku Tokyo 153 0064
Tel: (03) 5437 0171
Fax: (03) 5437 0755

Asia Pacific
Berkeley Books LTD
5 Little Road #08-01
Singapore 536983
Tel: (65) 280-1330
Fax: (65) 280-6290

First edition
07 06 05 04 03 02 01   10 9 8 7 6 5 4 3 2 1

Design by Gopa and the Bear

Printed in the United States of America

To my students

CONTENTS

INTRODUCTION

THIS SMALL BOOK of meditations is for anyone who longs to put their compassion into action, to make compassion real in everyday ways. It is for those who want to balance caring for self and caring for the world, because they recognize that the health of the human psyche and the health of the world are inextricably related, and we cannot truly heal one without healing the other. And it is for those who understand that to deepen in compassion we need to open our hearts and face the suffering inside ourselves and in the world around us, because when we face suffering with an open heart we find

1

momentary pain but we also find the doorway to lasting fulfillment and freedom.

These meditations are based on my book *The Rhythm of Compassion: Caring for Self, Connecting with Society,* which uses the metaphor of the in-breath and the out-breath to help people balance care of self and others. There is a natural time for the in-breath of caring for self and family, and a natural time for the out-breath of caring for the needs of the world. The challenge is to become skillful in following your rhythm of compassion—knowing when it is time to go inward and when to go out into the community.

These short meditations are designed to help you learn to follow your unique rhythm of compassion. In part, the meditations are inspired by the most frequent questions and concerns expressed in the many letters and e-mails I have received and from the people who have read *The Rhythm of Compassion* and attended my lectures.

✦ What are the most effective tools for balancing caring for self and others?

✦ How do I find the courage to face suffering—my own, my family's, and my community's?

✦ How do I find the time to serve, or the time to care for myself?

✦ How do I know when I've done enough for the person I care for?

✦ What helps when the suffering of the world overwhelms me?

✦ How do I cultivate genuine compassion rather than moral do-goodism?

3

Though these questions came from a remarkably diverse cross-section of people—ministers, social workers, teachers, parents, therapists, business executives and managers, college students, activists, and healers—what they all had in common was a yearning to deepen in compassion and a recognition that their own health was inseparable from the health of the world.

Circle of Compassion is designed for you to incorporate into your chosen spiritual practice. The book is divided into four parts with several sets of meditations within each part, as well as a brief introduction on the specific purpose behind each part. I suggest working with one meditation a day. Start by gently following the pathway of your in-breath, and then your out-breath. Notice how much your breath can teach you about how to balance inner and outer. Continue gently following your breath until your mind becomes calm and receptive. Then read the meditation several times, letting the words enter your consciousness. If you follow this time of focusing on the meditation with a period of stillness, the words will settle in you at a deeper level. Sometimes you may want to return to a meditation several times during the day, or work with an especially relevant meditation for several days.

I suggest working your way through all the meditations first, as this lays the foundation for finding and following your rhythm of compassion. Then I invite you to use the meditations in a more spontaneous way. For instance, if you know you are tired or reaching burn-out, you can turn to Part Two, "The In-Breath: Caring for Self," and allow the "Claiming Self-Care" meditations to guide you toward self-renewal. Maybe you feel overwhelmed as you care for an aging parent or difficult coworker, then turning to Part

Three, "The Out-Breath: Caring for the World," and the meditations in "Cultivating the Four Qualities of Mature Compassion" can help you to continue caring for these people in a tender and skillful way. Or perhaps you are deeply concerned about caring for the earth, then you might turn to the meditations in "Practicing Mature Compassion for the Earth" and learn about ecological mindfulness.

My hope is that by using the simple meditations in this book, you will learn to integrate your rhythm so your inner self-care helps you serve the world, and your caring for the world contributes to your soul. I believe that both our own well-being and the well-being of the planet depend on how skillfully we practice this integration.

PART I

LEARNING TO FOLLOW
YOUR RHYTHM OF COMPASSION

*The time for contemplation is the spring that
feeds our action, and our action will be as
deep as the spring. We need time to allow the
spirit to clear the obstacles—the clinging
debris and mud—that keeps the spring from
flowing freely from its clear, deep source.
And we need time for the spring to overflow
into insightful and compassionate action.*

—Thomas Merton

PART ONE, "Learning to Follow Your Rhythm of Compassion," lays the foundation for the rest of the book to build upon. The first set of meditations, "Nurturing Your Spiritual Practice," focuses on daily spiritual practice as the strongest foundation for compassion. It is in the stillness of your practice—be it meditation, prayer, yoga, or time in nature—that you can hear your rhythm breathing in and out and find the spaciousness to hold the complexity of suffering. To further build a solid foundation for compassion, the next meditations, "Confronting the Trickster Busyness" and "Belonging to Your Place," guide you to clear away the busyness and unneeded aspects of your life to make room for what really matters and to create a strong sense of place where you live as the literal grounding for your rhythm of compassion. Finally, in the last section of this part, you are introduced to the friends of compassion—imagination, discipline, and support—to help make compassion real in your daily life.

Nurturing Your Spiritual Practice

The fruit of silence is prayer,
The fruit of prayer is faith,
The fruit of faith is love, and
The fruit of love is silence.

—Mother Teresa

My particular rhythm of compassion tells me when it's time to breathe in, caring for myself, and when it's time to breathe out, caring for the world. I commit to creating the conditions in my life that allow me to honor my rhythm.

In order to hear my rhythm I dedicate myself to a spiritual practice that helps me reconnect with my spirit, quiet my mind, and open my heart.

I take time to find the practice that works best for me—sitting on a meditation cushion, kneeling in prayer, breathing with a yoga posture, reading a spiritual text, or spending quiet time in nature. I choose my practice and I nurture it daily.

If needed, I seek a teacher or class to guide me in finding the spiritual practice that suits me best. This guidance helps me dedicate myself to my practice. Like me, many people need support in finding and dedicating themselves to their chosen practice.

Today I recommit to creating the space in my life for connecting with my spirit, quieting my mind, and opening my heart. Even if a few minutes of quiet are all I can find, I have planted the seeds of my commitment. A few minutes dedicated to spirit go a long way.

Nurturing my spiritual practice is a gift not just to myself but also to all the people I care for in my life. My family, my colleagues, and my friends all benefit from my growing peace of mind and open heart that come from practice.

As I quiet myself today I focus on Meister Eckhart's beautiful words: "There is nothing in the universe that resembles God so much as silence."

My spiritual practice is the quiet space from which
I listen to my rhythm. This time of silence and solitude
is the very heartbeat of my rhythm of compassion.

As I learn to listen to my rhythm of compassion I find my balance between caring for myself and caring for the world. I am learning to balance a rich inner life and a passionate engagement with the world.

Right now, I stop and breathe in the quiet.

Right now, being present to this moment

is the possibility for my awakening.

Confronting the Trickster Busyness

The rush and pressure of modern life are a form,
perhaps the most common form, of innate violence.
To allow oneself to be carried away by a multitude of
conflicting concerns, to surrender to too many demands,
to commit oneself to too many projects, to want to help
everyone in everything is to succumb to violence.
The frenzy of the activist neutralizes his work for peace.
It destroys her own inner capacity for peace. It kills
the root of inner wisdom which makes work fruitful.

—Thomas Merton

Constant busyness is a form of violence.

I acknowledge that too much busyness steals my

capacity for compassion toward both myself and others.

In the stillness of my practice I hear my rhythm
of compassion breathe in and out. I hear the call to help
teenagers, or protect the whales, or sit with the dying.
It's time to rest; I've done enough. Busyness is eating
me up; I need to stop and take a retreat.

Today I focus on Jacob Needleman's powerful words:
"The time famine of our lives and our culture is in fact
a symptom of metaphysical starvation."

I confront the trickster busyness as I eliminate the life activities that drain my energy and leave me feeling empty.

I clear away what I don't need in my life: too much work, television, the Internet, and stimulation; complaining and self-absorption; unnecessary dates and constantly doing for others.

I make room for what really matters to me—family and friends, good self-care, creativity, and contribution to my community

When I am alone driving in my car I use this as quiet time; I empty out, I pray, I remember what I am grateful for, I am quiet.

I ask my family for their support in giving me half
an hour of alone time each day. This is my sacred time:
I light a candle and pray; I sit quietly and listen to music;
I read my favorite poems or sacred passages;
or I do nothing.

I have the courage to clear away the social engagements that I really don't need, or the ones that leave me feeling empty and unfulfilled. I make space for what nourishes me.

I make room for long-forgotten and deeply felt dreams: a dance class; doing yoga; hiking and time in the natural world; playing soccer with my kids; volunteering at the local recycling center or at the hospital.

This weekend I unplug the phones.

I turn off my computer—enough e-mail and Internet.

I hike with my family, we read together, or just hang out

enjoying one another. If I am alone I take long walks,

cook my favorite meal, listen to my favorite symphony,

or have the luxury of longer time for meditation and

prayer. I come home to myself.

I make room to hear my rhythm of compassion.

Belonging to Your Place

We have forgotten what we can count on.
The natural world provides refuge. . . .
Each of us harbors a homeland,
a landscape we naturally comprehend.
By understanding the dependability of place,
we can anchor ourselves as trees.
—Terry Tempest Williams

I put down deep roots where I live. I belong to my place,
this is the very grounding for my rhythm of compassion.
This helps me belong to myself.

To create my sense of place I begin by becoming intimate with the particulars of my home landscape: the plants, creatures, stones, trees, buildings, landmarks, and people.

I create my sense of place as I walk every inch
of my surroundings, feed the birds, or plant gardens
of indigenous herbs.

Today I practice mindful intimacy with my place
as I stop and notice the subtle details of the sounds,
sights, smells, and textures that surround me.

This week I study the maps and history of my region. I am falling in love with my place. I write a love poem to my home landscape.

Over time I fall in love with the light and shadow
of the days and the cycles of the seasons. As I learn
to live in harmony with the cycles of my place,
I begin to live in harmony with my own seasons
and my own light and shadow.

Today I focus on Terry Tempest Williams's wise words about place: "Each of us harbors a homeland, a landscape we naturally comprehend. By understanding the dependability of place, we can anchor ourselves as trees."

There are few things in life as steadfast as my place. It is my ground for meaning. As I belong to my place, I belong to myself. I am rooted in my rhythm knowing when to pay attention to myself, and when to focus on the world.

Cultivating the Friends of Compassion:
Imagination, Discipline, and Support

> *It is compassion that removes the heavy bar,*
> *opens the door to freedom, makes the narrow*
> *heart as wide as the world. Compassion*
> *takes away from the heart the inert weight,*
> *the paralyzing heaviness; it gives wings*
> *to those who cling to the lowlands of self.*
> —Nyanaponika Thera

The qualities of imagination, discipline, and support are the friends of compassion helping me find and sustain my rhythm.

Today I follow my imagination as it guides me toward my unique ingredients for balancing inner and outer. My imagination asks me what forms of self-renewal most nourish and renew me? What forms of service are calling to me and asking me to open my heart?

Following my rhythm of compassion is a rich creative process. My imagination guides me as I experiment with different kinds of self-renewal and new forms of service to my community until I find the right fit.

Today my imagination gets me out of the box and shows me how to combine quality of life with service to others. For example, my family volunteers together at a soup kitchen or planting trees; or my coworkers and I set up a recycling program at work, or volunteer to mentor teens.

Discipline is a friend who helps me clear away space for what matters to me and take a stand for my quality of life. Discipline is my rhythm with a purpose.

Today my discipline helps me eliminate at least one unnecessary activity—a phone call, meeting, errand, e-mail, an item on my to-do list, or an obligation to someone else. I protect this time for some form of self-renewal.

With the help of discipline—my rhythm with a purpose—
I commit to clear away at least one unnecessary activity
each day for the next month. By taking one step at a time
I learn to make space for the things that matter to me.

To care for myself and others I need support. It is my highest priority to build my support network through friends, family, colleagues, therapists, mentors, or support groups. I understand that this support is what fuels and sustains my compassion for both myself and the world.

I know that I can't grow alone. I need the reflection of those who support me in order to see both my light and my shadow.

The next time I feel stressed or overwhelmed at home or at work, I reach out and ask for help. I remember I don't have to go it alone. I remember compassion involves many hands and many hearts.

Part II
The In-Breath: Caring for Self

Friend, hope for the truth while you are alive.

Jump into experience while you are alive!

Think . . . and think . . . while you are alive.

What you call "salvation" belongs

to the time before death.

If you don't break your ropes while you're alive,

do you think ghosts will do it after?

—Kabir

It's surprising how many of us don't take care of ourselves. We're too busy working; or taking care of others is always first and we're always last; or we might feel that saving the world is too urgent and there's not really time for self-care. But the truth is that without self-care we cannot sustain high-quality work, take care of our families and loved ones, or make a lasting difference in the world. The in-breath of caring for self is the doorway to true mature compassion. The next meditations guide you to claim self-care as an essential aspect of a spiritually vital and socially engaged life. They invite you to fearlessly heal yourself because when you face your own suffering a genuine compassion for all of life awakens within you.

Claiming Self-Care

*More and more people are tired of the fast-paced, frenzied
"information age" and are interested in higher-quality
lives—lives in which they have more time for themselves
and their relationships, more energy to invest in their
emotional, physical, and spiritual well-being.*

—Cheryl Richardson

Caring for myself is essential for my physical, mental, emotional, and spiritual well-being. I claim self-care as central to a spiritually vital and socially engaged life. My in-breath of self-care is a time to empty out; a time to find fresh perspective; a time to dream, reflect, and reprioritize about what matters to me.

Right now I stop, I breathe in. I ask, What can I do to take better care of my self?

This month I make time to explore the forms of self-renewal that most nourish me: poetry or dance, silent retreat, time in the mountains or by the sea, long-distance running, reading or solitude, singing in a choir or playing an instrument.

A small dose of self-renewal goes a long way in restoring me. This week I take an afternoon of silence and solitude, a day of hiking in the earth's beauty, some time to share deeply with dear friends, or an evening of music.

During my in-breath of self-care I nurture the spiritual values—patience, loving-kindness, courage, and strength—that sustain me and empower me to move skillfully into the world.

My in-breath of self-care is the doorway to true mature compassion. When I care for myself I am preparing the ground to care for my family, my work, and the world.

Today I focus on this simple truth: To be kind to another

I need to be kind to myself.

Healing Yourself:
The Heart of Self-Care

A man has many skins in himself,
covering the depths of his heart.
Man knows so many things;
he does not know himself.
Why, thirty or forty skins or hides,
just like an ox's or a bear's so thick and hard,
cover the soul. Go into your own ground
and learn to know yourself there.
—Meister Eckhart

The deepest level of my self-care is fearlessly facing *all* the parts of myself and making a commitment to heal my wounded and defended parts.

I begin healing myself with this commitment to tell
the truth: I confront my fears; I find where I am defended;
and I face the pain from which I am hiding.

Today I focus on Marion Woodman's words as she gives me courage to fearlessly face all the parts of myself: "In finding our own story, we assemble all the parts of ourselves. Whatever kind of mess we have made of it, we can somehow see the totality of who we are and recognize how our blunderings are related. We can own what we did and value who we are, not because of the outcome, but because of the soul story that propelled us."

When needed, I seek help from a therapist, teacher, or support group to guide me through my healing journey. I know that healing myself is a balance of solitude and support from others.

Today I take Thomas Merton's wise words into my heart: "The truth that many people never understand until it's too late, is that the more you avoid suffering, the more you suffer."

I learn to embrace my difficulties as spiritual
challenges that shape me and make me deeply human.
I learn that when I can go toward the things
that frighten me, then I am free.

Today I see that my fears, inadequacies, and pain are the
very feelings that connect me to the heart of the world.
I see that my tears are part of the *lacrimae rerum*,
the tears that are in things. I see that there is no need
to hide these parts of myself.

I understand that by facing my own suffering I learn
true compassion. As I face the difficult parts of myself,
a genuine compassion for all of life awakens within me.

Entering the Deepest Waters
of Self-Compassion

Being human and ordinary, we will often fail
to love the whole, the dark and difficult parts.
We will always try to avoid something.
We will tremble. We will be blind.
We will be uncertain. We will continue to hurt
one another and miss the essential.
We will always need mercy and compassion.
—Gunilla Norris

With time my healing journey takes me into deeper waters asking me to learn compassion for the darkest parts of myself: my false mask that I use to hide my true self; my core wound that keeps me stuck in self-destructive behaviors; my secret shadow parts that I am ashamed to admit even to myself. Slowly, like the gentle blossoming of a flower, I find compassion for my deepest suffering.

Right now I stop, I breathe in. I ask, What is the darkest part of my suffering that I need to bring out into the light of my compassion?

I understand that my heart opens gradually to my deepest suffering. Moment by moment, petal by petal, my heart comes into full blossom. I cannot will or force this opening; rather, I gently offer my readiness to face the truth.

Today I take one simple step, I stay present to the pain inside me. Sadness, fear, confusion, frustration—I simply notice. I don't run away.

I have the inner strength to feel the pain of my broken heart, the place where I am most shattered and hurt. I stay open to my brokenness, and through this courageous opening I receive the teaching and the healing of my broken heart.

Today, as I face my brokenness, I find comfort in Meister Eckhart's words: "Truly, it is in the darkness that one finds the light, so when we are in sorrow, then the light is nearest of all to us."

I take the pieces of my brokenness and I create something new and meaningful. I offer this wisdom to others. Now I understand that my very brokenness is my connection to the unbroken whole.

I have nothing to hide or defend; I offer the pain of my wounds and the fragility of my brokenness. The door of my heart is wide open; this is the door of compassion for myself and the world.

I have opened my heart to my own suffering, and now
I am ready to keep my heart open to the world's suffering.
I realize that compassion is a living circle starting with
myself and now going out to meet the world.

I nurture and care for myself. I become ripe like a fruit tree. I am ready to offer my fullness to the world.

PART III

THE OUT-BREATH: CARING FOR THE WORLD

*During my years of being close to people engaged in
changing the world I have seen fear turn into courage.
Sorrow into joy. Funerals into celebration. Because
whatever the consequences, people, standing side by side,
have expressed who they really are, and that ultimately
they believe in the love of the world and each other
enough to be that—which is the foundation of activism.*

—Alice Walker

ALL SPIRITUAL TRADITIONS emphasize the mutually beneficial interchange between self-fulfillment and service to others —the in-breath and the out-breath. At the heart of this wisdom is the simple and profound understanding that we cannot ignore others' suffering because they are part of us. If we isolate ourselves and disconnect from the suffering in the world we are actually disconnecting from ourselves. This fragmentation is at the core of our spiritual emptiness in America today. These next meditations invite you to expand your circle of compassion to include all of life—old and young, vital and dying, familiar and strange, humans and creatures, forests and rivers. They guide you to choose your path of service carefully and to cultivate the four qualities of mature compassion that help you become skillful in caring for other people and the earth. As you breathe out, opening to the immensity of the world's pain, you open to the immensity of the compassion within you.

Preparing to Care for Others

I slept and dreamt that life was joy,
I woke and found that life was service,
I acted and, behold, service was joy.
—Rabindranath Tagore

My rhythm of compassion is breathing out, leading me toward the world. I take quiet time and ask: What form of service is calling me? What do I long to give back to the world?

Today I make a list of all the different talents I can offer as I serve. This helps me wisely choose my path of service.

As I start out on my path of service I remember to engage in something I enjoy, and to start small, being careful not to overcommit myself.

Sometimes finding my path of giving is a creative process of trial and error. I embrace this very process as a rich part of my learning. This month I take time to research the path that's right for me: mentoring troubled teens, serving the dying, working with prisoners, cleaning up a river, helping in an animal shelter, or spending time with the elderly.

Today I focus on Dr. Martin Luther King's beautiful words:

"Everyone can be great because everyone can serve."

After the honeymoon phase of falling in love with my service, I might notice some of these more complicated feelings arising within me: my need for approval or status; my fear, boredom, or perfectionism; a martyr complex that says I can never do enough; or the shame and guilt that motivate my service. I take time to identify my shadow.

I pause, I breathe in, I make space to hold my contradictions. I acknowledge that right next to my genuine desire to serve sits my shadow side.

I bring my shadow out into the bright light of my awareness. I talk and laugh about it with others—they all have shadows, too. If needed, I get help from a therapist or support group. All of this transforms my shadow.

As I find my true path of service and stay aware of the shadow side of my motivation, more and more my giving arises from a spontaneous generosity and the natural joy of serving.

Cultivating the Four Qualities
of Mature Compassion

Compassion in action is paradoxical and mysterious.
It is absolute yet continually changing. It accepts that
everything is happening exactly as it should, and it
works with a full-hearted commitment to change.
It is joyful in the midst of suffering, and hopeful
in the face of overwhelming odds. It is simple in
a world of complexity and confusion. It is done for
others, but it nurtures the self. It intends to eliminate
suffering, knowing that suffering is limitless.
—Ram Dass

Sometimes, as I care for my sick child or my frail and aging parent, a person with AIDS or a battered woman, a poisoned river or an abused creature, the suffering overwhelms me and questions flood my heart. Does my caring matter? Can I ever do enough? How can I get away from all this suffering? How do I act in these painful situations? These brave and difficult questions open the door to a fuller, more mature compassion.

Quieting my mind through my chosen spiritual practice
is the first step toward a more mature compassion.
Like a still lake, my quiet mind allows me to see beyond
the surface of suffering. Deep in the stillness I see that
I cannot fix, or change, or control the suffering around
me. Deep in the stillness I can hold both my intention to
alleviate suffering and my acceptance of it just as it is.

Today when I encounter the pain of my child, partner, colleague, or friend, I pause, I breathe in, I quiet my mind. Deep in the stillness I see clearly there is no need to change or fix their pain. I am a still lake for them.

As my mind becomes quiet, I begin to hear the gentle voice of my heart. My heart reminds me of its vast reservoirs of loving-kindness and courage that I can draw from as I encounter the suffering of the world. The gentle voice of my heart whispers all suffering is the same—yours, mine, society's, and the earth's—there is no use trying to avoid the ocean you are part of.

Today, as I practice opening my heart, I remember Jack Kornfield's words: "To open deeply, as genuine spiritual life requires, we need tremendous courage and strength, a kind of warrior spirit. But the place of this warrior strength is in the heart."

My quiet mind and open heart prepare the ground for my presence to emerge. Presence assures me there's no need to worry about performing or "doing the right thing" as I care for others. Just be myself. Presence allows my caring to always be a mutual exchange where I heal, and I am healed.

Today I practice presence as I care for those around me. I am myself as I listen, laugh, cry, and share joys and sorrows. The boundaries between giver and receiver disappear.

From presence emerges radical simplicity. In the midst
of the immense complexity of the world's suffering,
my service is radically simple. I do whatever small thing
is needed in a given moment with a loving heart.
This radical simplicity helps me when I feel overwhelmed
by suffering.

The next time some form of suffering overwhelms me
I remember to practice radical simplicity. I remember
Mother Teresa's words: "One cannot do great things,
one can only do small things with great love."

As I cultivate a quiet mind, an open heart, presence, and radical simplicity, my compassion deepens and matures. My mature compassion finds unity in seeming contradictions—joy in the midst of suffering, peaceful acceptance combined with passionate engagement, and hope in the face of complex challenges.

Practicing Mature Compassion
for the Human Family

If while we practice, we are not aware that the world is suffering, that children are dying of hunger, that social injustice is going on a little bit everywhere, we are not practicing mindfulness. We are just trying to escape.

—Thich Nhat Hanh

As my compassion matures I see the unclouded truth—
suffering is everywhere—in myself, my family,
my community, my society, and the earth itself.
To deepen in compassion I learn to accept and stay open
to the universality of suffering.

To help me stay open I turn to my chosen spiritual practice—prayer, meditation, yoga, time in nature, or a long talk with a trusted friend or counselor—to remind me that I can't control or fix suffering, but I can be present to it. To remind me that in our suffering we're all the same.

Today I focus on this lovely teaching from Sharon Salzberg: "The goal of our spiritual practice is to be able to understand, to be able to look without illusion at what is natural in this life, at what is actually happening for others and for ourselves. This willingness to see what is true is the first step in developing compassion."

I understand that as I genuinely accept the universal presence of suffering, I am also accepting responsibility for engaged action. As I embrace this paradox of acceptance and responsibility, I strengthen my capacity for caring.

Today, as I encounter the suffering of someone I help—
my child or parent, client or colleague, friend or stranger—
I quiet my mind and open my heart. I breathe in their
suffering with the wish that they be free of pain, and
I breathe out sending them love and healing. And again,
I breathe in their suffering with the wish that they be free
of pain, and I breathe out sending them love and healing.
I use this simple and powerful practice whenever I need it.

In some situations of profound suffering—a friend or family member who is dying, serving someone in prison, a young person with AIDS, or a woman who has been raped—the pain is so great it breaks my heart. In these situations I practice staying open to the suffering and letting the pain break my heart.

Today I focus on the phrase "my heart is breaking, my heart is awakening." As I care for others, my heart shatters, and so does the hard shell of my ego. My broken heart awakens me and liberates me.

I know that heartbreak is an inevitable part of compassion.
It opens me and deeply connects me to those I serve.
As I tend to a child with cancer, a parent with Alzheimer's,
a victim of unspeakable child abuse, or an innocent victim
of random gun violence—I surround myself with the
phrase "my heart is breaking, my heart is awakening."
This reminds me that each time my heart breaks it also
grows strong and luminous.

Right now I stop, I breathe in. I imagine my heart of compassion in full blossom. No defending, no fixing, avoiding, or intellectualizing the suffering of the world. My heart is fully open. I am fully alive.

I truly understand that to abandon others in their
suffering is to abandon myself.
To open to the immensity of others' pain
is to open to the immense compassion within me.

Practicing Mature Compassion for the Earth

*Asking what good are eagles and owls,
or ebony spleenworts, or black-footed ferrets, or
snail darters, or any other of our fellow travelers,
is like asking what good are our brothers and
sisters, or children, or friends. Such questions
arise only in the absence of love.*

—Scott Russell Sanders

My compassion for the earth begins when I recognize that my destiny is profoundly linked with the fate of the earth. The way I live today affects the future of all living things. Indeed, the health of my soul and the health of the planet is a seamless continuum.

Today I focus on the significance of James Hillman's words: "Psychology, so dedicated to awakening human consciousness, needs to wake up to one of the most ancient human truths: we cannot be studied or cured apart from the planet."

Like all compassion, ecological compassion begins at home as I plant a garden and compost; conserve water in my kitchen and bathroom; recycle, reuse, and repair; and every time I shop with green values. Each of these is an act of caring for the earth. I commit to at least one conscious act of ecological compassion every day.

Today I recognize my stewardship as a spiritual practice. Each earth-friendly act—recycling, car pooling, eco-wise shopping, conserving—is also an act of ecological mindfulness. Sustainable living offers me ongoing practice in mindfulness.

The degree of mindfulness that I bring to my most ordinary acts of sustainable living determines the sacredness in my daily life. My recycling bins become daily rounds of earth awareness; the water and energy I save are prayers of gratitude; the rides I share are a collective offering to clean fresh air. My mindfulness transforms the mundane into the sacred.

Just as I did with the human family, I stay open to the suffering of the earth family. My warrior heart feels, connects, and breaks as I encounter strangled rivers, raped forests, battered wetlands, or abused creatures. I breathe in their suffering with the wish that they be free of pain, and I breathe out sending them love and healing. And again, I breathe in their suffering with the wish that they be free of pain, and I breathe out sending them love and healing. I use this simple and powerful practice whenever I need it.

My awakened heart makes visible the suffering of
the earth—poisoned air and water, the abuse of over
development, the multitude of endangered species.
The more I open my heart to feel the pain, the more
connected, courageous, and alive I feel. I understand the
intimate connection between passion and compassion.

I know that there are no simple formulas for ecological compassion. I know that I cannot fix or control the vast suffering of the earth. But I can open wide the door of my heart, and respond to what's needed with lovingkindness and full engagement.

I understand that true stewardship is a partnership between reverence and responsibility.

Today, Mary Oliver's words ring at the very core of my being: "Each form sets a tone, enables a destiny, strikes a note in the universe unlike any other. How can we ever stop looking? How can we ever turn away?"

Caring for the earth puts me in harmony with a vast, eternal rhythm of compassion that cares not just for us, not just for now, but for the earth and all its future inhabitants. I open my circle of compassion and welcome the creatures, mountains, water, air, and forests. I know we are all wild and mysterious creatures with invisible threads connecting us in both our joy and our suffering.

PART IV

IN HARMONY WITH
YOUR RHYTHM OF COMPASSION

*I live my life in growing orbits
that move out over the things of the world.
Perhaps I can never achieve the last,
but that will be my attempt.*

*I am circling around God, around the ancient tower,
and I have been circling for a thousand years,
and I still don't know if I am a falcon, or a storm,
or a great song.*

—Rainer Maria Rilke

THESE FINAL MEDITATIONS reinforce the qualities that help you sustain your rhythm of compassion over time: coming full circle from the first meditations back to your spiritual practice; using your awareness to navigate both the light and shadow of the inner life and the life of service; and learning to trust the natural cycles of your rhythm. The last set of meditations reflects the cycle where, as you live more and more in harmony with your rhythm, the inner and the outer become indistinguishable. As inner and outer unite as one, your compassion comes into full blossom. Your relationship to your own suffering comes into proper perspective and you see how it fits within the larger web of life. Now you understand that what you have compassion for inside yourself, you can have compassion for out in the world. What you reject out in the world is also what you reject inside yourself. The full circle of compassion is alive within you, breathing in and breathing out.

Cultivating the Sustainers of Compassion: Spiritual Practice, Awareness, and Trust

> *There is nobody on the planet, neither those whom*
> *we see as the oppressed nor those whom we see*
> *as the oppressor, who doesn't have what it takes*
> *to wake up. . . . The source of all wakefulness,*
> *the source of all kindness and compassion, the*
> *source of all wisdom, is in each second of time.*
> —Pema Chodron

Dedication to my chosen spiritual practice is the key to sustain and deepen my compassion. My practice gives me the courage to open my heart and face life's suffering— my own, my family's, my community's, and the earth's. In the stillness of practice I hear my rhythm of compassion breathe in and breathe out. I hear how to balance caring for myself and caring for the world.

Right now I stop, I breathe in, I reconnect with my spirit, quiet my mind, and open my heart. Right now I am awake.

I cultivate awareness through regular spiritual practice.

My awareness allows me to recognize both the light

and shadow of the inner life and the outer life of service.

Awareness isn't a judgment; awareness is

a compassionate witness.

My awareness illuminates the positive nature of my
in-breath of self-care: time to reflect, clear out, dream,
find compassion for my own suffering and brokenness,
and time to heal. And my awareness illuminates the
potential shadow of my inner life: the dead end of
narcissism and self-absorption, becoming addicted
to my suffering, or creating my entire identity from
my wounds. Right now, what is the light and shadow
of my inner life?

My awareness illuminates the positive nature of my out-breath of service: a sense of purpose and fulfillment, a feeling of connection to the greater whole, the blossoming of generosity and compassion, and a fearless heart in the face of suffering. And my awareness illuminates the potential shadow of my life of service: my need to fix or control suffering; my unspoken desire for approval, status, or power; or being motivated by compulsive do-goodism, perfectionism, or looking better than others. Right now, what is the light and shadow of my life of service?

To sustain my rhythm of compassion I use my awareness
to skillfully navigate both the light and shadow of the
inner and outer. When I am in the shadow territory
it's a signal that I have lost the harmony in my rhythm.
Gently, awareness helps bring me back into balance.

I learn to trust the natural cycles of my rhythm of compassion. Sometimes my cycle takes me inward toward self-healing; sometimes I am completely outward serving the world; and other cycles find me balancing both the in-breath and the out-breath. My rhythm is inherent, already inside me, just waiting for me to listen and trust.

Trusting my cycles comes from the wisdom of a fully lived life: facing my fears and challenges and then getting on with it; finding what I love and doing it; and offering what I've learned to the world.

I follow my rhythm by cultivating the sustainers
of compassion—spiritual practice, awareness, and trust.
This trinity keeps me in balance, breathing in
and breathing out.

Uniting Inner and Outer

*The labyrinth is thoroughly known. We have only
to follow the thread of the hero path, and where
we had thought to find an abomination, we shall
find a god. And where we had thought to slay another,
we shall slay ourselves. Where we had thought
to travel outward, we will come to the center
of our own existence. And where we had thought
to be alone, we will be with all the world.*

—Joseph Campbell

I know that my own health is inseparable from the health of the world, and that I cannot truly heal one without healing the other. In my quest for wholeness I balance my yearning for self-fulfillment with service to others.

My in-breath of self-care gives me the clear mind and open heart that I need to face the complex challenges of the world. My in-breath of self-care is essential to sustaining my engagement with the world. The outer must have the inner.

The gifts I receive from my out-breath of caring for the world are precious contributions to own my development. I am healed in profound and mysterious ways through serving others. My out-breath of service is essential to my personal healing and wholeness. The inner must have the outer.

As my inner and outer unite as one, my compassion comes into full blossom. My relationship to my own suffering comes into proper perspective and I see how it fits within the larger web of life. Now I see the true nature of suffering and I can respond skillfully to it. Now I see that entering the heart of suffering causes momentary pain, but gives me lasting fulfillment.

As my inner and outer unify, I can get out of the way and do less, so that a greater presence can flow through me and accomplish more. Working in partnership with this divine presence gives me the courage and support to respond to more of the world's challenges. I fortify this divine partnership through my spiritual practice.

In the seamless unity of inner and outer I understand that what I have compassion for inside myself, I can have compassion for out in the world. What I reject out in the world is also what I reject inside myself.

In a moment of absolute stillness during spiritual practice, I feel as if I am actively encountering the suffering of the world. And in a moment of intense engaged caring for someone, I feel utterly still as if I am praying. The boundaries between inner and outer have disappeared.

Today I consider this teaching about the unity of inner and outer from Liu I-Ming in *Awakening to the Tao:* "When the inward and the outward are illumined, and all is clear, you are one with the light of sun and moon. When developed to its ultimate state, this is a round luminosity which nothing can deceive, the subtle body of a unified spirit, pervading the whole universe."

I am in harmony with my rhythm of compassion.

I am in tune with a great universal cadence where

a rich inner life is exquisitely balanced with a passionate

engagement with the world. I have come home to myself.

I am at home both in the small intimate house of my

own belonging, as well as belonging to the immensity

of the house of the world.

FOR FURTHER SUPPORT

For more extended meditations and for the fullest understanding of the ideas in this book we recommend Gail Straub's
*The Rhythm of Compassion: Caring for Self, Connecting
with Society*, Tuttle Publishing. Contact your bookstore,
on-line store, or Tuttle Publishing at 800-526-2778.

For further information on Gail Straub's trainings, books,
and audio cassettes contact:

EMPOWERMENT TRAINING PROGRAMS
1649 Rt.28A , West Hurley, New York, 12491
Fax: 845-331-3041
E-mail: gstraub@empowermenttraining.com
Website: www.empowermenttraining.com

Also by Gail Straub
from Journey Editions / Tuttle Publishing

The Rhythm of Compassion
Caring for Self, Connecting with Society

ISBN 1-885203-83-7 (hardcover)
ISBN 1-58290-058-2 (paperback)

An essential book for anyone lost in the mire of personal wounds
or burned out from taking care of others.
Gail Straub writes, "The health of the human psyche and the health
of the world are inextricably related, and we cannot truly heal
one without healing the other."

AVAILABLE FROM YOUR LOCAL BOOKSTORE
OR
DIRECT FROM TUTTLE PUBLISHING
800-526-2778
(CREDIT CARD ORDERS ONLY)